I SEE YOU!

MARSHA L. JONES

© 2025
IBG Publications, Inc.
www.ibgpublications.com

Published by I.B.G. Publications, Inc., A Power to Wealth Company
Web address: www.ibgpublications.com
admin@ibgpublications.com / 904-419-9810
Copyright, 2025 by Marsha L. Jones
IBG Publications, Inc., Orange Park, FL
ISBN: 978-1-956266-92-4

Jones, Marsha L.
I See You!

All rights reserved. This book, or its parts may not be reproduced in any form, stored in a retrieval system, or transmitted in any form, by any means-electronic, mechanical, photocopy, recording or otherwise, without prior written permission of the publisher or author, except as provided by the United States of America Copyright law.

All scriptures are from the Kings James version of the Bible unless otherwise noted.

Printed in the United States of America.

DEDICATION

     This book is dedicated to my Lord and Savior, Jesus Christ. He is my Keeper.

     "The Lord will keep you from all harm, he will watch over your life. The Lord will watch over your coming and going both now and forevermore."
--Psalm 121:8 NIV

     To my loving sister, Denise, a sensitive and experienced Registered Nurse, who heard my distressful voice and saved my life with emphatic and urgent instructions: "Do it now!"

     To my dearly departed husband, Wiley, who was the finest of all coaches, the-crème de la crème. He saw my potential, looked into my heart, and brought the best out of me. He encouraged and supported me to the utmost. He stood beside me through it all, in sickness and in health. He was my best and faithful friend, loyal supporter, wise instructor, and the love of my life.

"The Lord will keep you from all harm, he will watch over your life. The Lord will watch over your coming and going both now and forevermore."
—Psalm 121:8 NIV

ACKNOWLEDGMENTS

It's my honor to gratefully acknowledge those who've played invaluable positive roles in my life and who continue to be true friends and an inspiration. I'm truly blessed and thankful to you all, including many of you who've also been encouraging and supportive in me writing this book that hopefully blesses and inspires all who read it to trust God.

To my beautiful and brilliant daughter, Melanie, who continues to encourage me by singing gospel songs and speaking godly wisdom.

To my handsome and caring son, Michael, who supports me and helps to make the load lighter.

To my beautiful and perspective, daughter-in-love, Kimberly, who is sensitive to my wants and desires.

To my beautiful and devoted sister, Sheila, who is my inspiration.

To my treasured and compassionate friends, Pastors Curtis and Joyce Levi, whose prayers are greatly appreciated.

To my dear and kindhearted friend, Pastor Dorothy Porter, whose words of comfort are still ringing in my ears.

To my beautiful and illustrious editor, Flo Jenkins, whose expertise, and knowledge are a treasure.

TABLE OF CONTENTS

DEDICATION………..……..…………………………....3
ACKNOWLEDGMENTS……………………………….5
PREFACE……………………………………………......9

DAY 1…Do It Now!..16

DAY 2…Nurse Comfort.. Jesus Can Work It Out…………….....22

DAY 3...Nurse Patience "I Will Never Leave You Nor Forsake You".26

DAY 4…Jasmine… "PYT" (Pretty Young Thing) …………….…..32

DAY 5…God's Grace………………………………………………36

DAY 6…The Sunflower. Precious Memories…..………………….40

DAY 7…Pushing Through The Pain- "Strong & Fast" ……………44

DAY 8…God Keeps His Promises……………………………..….48

DAY 9…Jesus... The Light Of The World!..................................54

DAY 10…God Already Worked It Out!..58

DAY 11…Home At Last!..62

Oct. 2019…Time To Downsize……………………………………..66

Nov. 2019…God's Plan Works Best……………………………….70

Dec 2019…True Acts Of God……………………………………..74

Jan 2020…It Was My Voice… It Was Me!................................78

Feb 2020…The GREATEST Of These Is LOVE!...............................82

May 2020...Divine Connection..86

June 2020...A Forever Faithful God.................................…..........90

Credits...Credits..….................93

Meet The Author...95
Other Books By The Author...97

PREFACE

Oftentimes, I think of my life as an adventurous journey! I have met wonderful acquaintances along the way—many who have become faithful, longtime friends throughout the years.

My journey started in rural Indiana on a farm. Milking cows, gathering eggs, and tending to the garden were daily chores. At the end of the day when the sun was setting, I would look out into the horizon and wonder what people would be doing in California where it would still be daylight. I was looking beyond the horizon, dreaming, and wondering about so many things. I was a child then.

Years later, I married the love of my life, Wiley. We were a married couple on a college campus. Wiley was granted a four-year football scholarship, which meant football practice during the week, game day on Saturday, and game reviews on Sunday.

In the cold, rainy, and snowy weather, I would bundle up our baby daughter, Melanie, and head to the football stadium. We were, indeed, a football family.

We lived in a manufactured home that measured 10 ft. wide and 50 ft. long. It was the size of a semi-trailer. Wiley pursued his career in education and coached college football for a season. He taught Health Science and coached football at his high school alma mater.

I obtained a Teller position in a nearby bank and continued my path in education in the public school district. When an opportunity for a career advancement opened in Texas, we left our roots, family and friends, and headed to Dallas, Texas. There, we were welcomed with good ol' Southern hospitality and mouthwatering Tex-Mex food. I discovered what was real Mexican food! (It was not what I was accustomed to: Taco Bell☺.) I devoured enchiladas and burritos. My favorite entrées were the sizzling hot, lip-smacking fajitas.

Yummy! It was delectable.

Moving to Texas not only introduced us to delicious food, but it also broadened our horizon. Leaving my countryside home—where my closest neighbor was a mile away and the town population was a little over 20,000—and moving to a big city with a population of one million folks was a major and challenging adjustment.

There were so many new encounters. Traffic on a freeway was jam-packed with cars, trucks, and semi-trucks whizzing by compared to the back roads of my farming community where tractors with plows and combines leisurely drove to the corn fields and soybean fields. Everything seemed to be fast-paced in Dallas.

Another adjustment was the Texas drawl and colloquialism. My children picked up a common Texas phrase of "fixin' to" and "y'all". I corrected them by saying those words were not in the dictionary. One day, my daughter came home and reported to me that it was all right to use those words, because the English teacher said, "Y'all get ready to leave, cause the bell fixin' to ring." Okay?

As far as sports go, in Indiana, basketball was king, now but in Texas, football was king. Yeehaw, Dallas Cowboys!

In the mind of a farmer's daughter, I saw us as being transplanted into warm, fertile soil. God was growing us. My viewpoint and ideas were expanding. Oh, my! What a wonder! We lived in Texas for 18 months. In pursuit of our dream, it was time to move on.

Wiley had a plan to be a lobbyist for teachers' rights and education. The plan was to cover different regions of the nation and eventually go to Washington, D.C. As a lobbyist, his goal was to influence elected officials to create legislation addressing rising educational and teacher issues across the nation.

We traveled from the Midwest to the Southwest, and we were now on our way to the Pacific West. Living in Southern California … A Dream Come True!

When we moved to Southern California, we fell in love with the climate, the beaches, the food, and the people. We immediately adapted to the climate. Compared to Indiana's cloudy and snowy winter weather, and the hot and humid Texas weather, California was a welcomed change. Ahh, now living in sunny Southern California weather—with nearby beaches bordering on the mighty Pacific Ocean—it was like paradise!

We made Southern California our home, living and loving the newness of it all. To me, it was like a dream come true. That little girl in Indiana who would look out the west window to watch the setting sun and wonder what people were doing in California was now a grown adult with a family living in the horizon of California. I still marvel at God's plan for my life.

I once heard a sermon about how life could be like a merry-go-round or like a roller coaster ride. It depends on your frame of mind. The analogy was that every day could be the same, like a merry-go-round, going around in a circle.

Boring. Nothing new. Every day doing the same ol' things, going to the same ol' job, seeing the same ol' people, and nothing changing. Or, our life could be like a roller coaster ride, with its ups and downs, loops and hoops, twist and turns. Exciting. Every day is a new day.

To quote author, Bill Keane, "Yesterday is history, tomorrow is a mystery, today is a gift of God, which is why we call it the present." Yes, indeed. It depends on our perspective and making quality decisions.

In our everyday life, sometimes our actions produce positive, optimist results, and sometimes our actions produce negative, detrimental results. In either case, God is always there. There is no mistake or difficulty so big that He cannot handle it. Our God is Omniscient, Omnipotent, and Omnipresent. Yes, we may suffer the consequences of our actions; yet, He gives us His mercy. For His mercies are new every morning. Great is His faithfulness.

—Lamentations 3:22-23

It is of the LORD'S mercies that we are not consumed, because his compassions fail not. *They are* new every morning: great *is* thy faithfulness.

–Lamentations 3:22-23 (KJV)

Wednesday, October 3, 2018:

6:45 a.m.

"DO IT NOW!"

"Call 911 … call the ambulance, Marsha, do it now! Get your ID, Insurance Cards, and your house keys. Do like I say. Do it now!" These were the lifesaving words from my sister, Denise. She is an experienced and skilled Registered Nurse of 30 years. Denise was emphatic and urgently demanding me to get to the hospital immediately.

You see, I got myself in trouble a few days earlier. On Sunday, I had a ravenous appetite.

I ate an enormous amount of savory Chinese food with jalapeños. I ate till I was full and fell asleep. About a half hour later, I woke up and ate some more. My appetite was insatiable!

I just could not get enough of this delicious spicy Chinese food. Yes, my mouth was burning, and my tastebuds were scorched.

When my tooth started aching, I knew I was in trouble. There was a blaze down in my gut. My stomach was on FIRE. I chugged a bottle of Pepto Bismol and guzzled several pints of water trying to extinguish the fire. I needed help.

I earnestly and humbly prayed, "Father God, forgive me for being gluttonous, and I promise I will never overeat again. Please take away this fire in my gut. I hurt myself. I am so sorry. Help me, please. Have mercy, Lord, in the name of Jesus. Amen."

Thank goodness the fire left, but now there was lingering pain growing more intense by the day. Tuesday night the pain was so severe that I was trembling and sweating. Every 30 minutes or so, I would convulse in pain.

This went on throughout the night. My husband, Wiley, suggested going to the hospital emergency room. I would have accepted it, but I knew Wiley had an early morning doctor's appointment and I did not want to jeopardize his meeting. Waiting in the emergency room would be an all-night affair.

Now, I desperately prayed, pleading that the Lord would remove the pain so I could sleep. In between the spasms of pain, I fell asleep exhausted. Thank you, Lord, for giving me a break and some sleep.

Here it is Wednesday morning, and I am on a prayer call. My sister, Denise, hears my voice on the phone. After the prayer, she calls me inquiring, "What is going on?

Your voice was noticeably different. You didn't sound like yourself." I told her what I had done and that I had been in pain for several days, since Sunday.

"This morning, I have excruciating pain, and my stomach is distended and hard." I was planning on going to the emergency room when my husband returned from his doctor's appointment. She exclaimed, "Don't Wait!"

That's when she gave me the instructions that saved my life.

"Call 911—call the ambulance, Marsha. Do it now. Get your ID, Insurance cards, and your house keys. Do like I say. Do it now!"

Because Denise was so insistent and demanding, it dawned upon me the severity of my condition. Without hesitation, I called 911. By the time I gathered all the information, the EMTs (Emergency Medical Technicians) were knocking at the door. Moving slowly with every agonizing step, I proceeded downstairs to let them in. I looked out the glass door and saw the ambulance parked at my front door.

I unlocked the door and the EMTs came rushing in like a flood. I turned around and sat down on my stair step. One EMT began taking my blood pressure, oxygen level, and heart rate. Another one was asking me questions about my condition and what medications I was taking. Two more were bringing in a gurney.

They were as busy as bees. Everyone had his own responsibility, and they worked together like a well-oiled machine. Oh, what a team. Thank God for EMTs. They were big, husky, muscular men, well equipped and able to lift me onto the gurney and swiftly wheel me into the ambulance. I felt safe and relieved as we traveled to Pomona Valley Hospital.

Upon arrival, X-rays of my abdomen were taken, which revealed gas and feces in my abdomen. I had a perforated bowel. I had become septic. Emergency surgery was urgent.

The surgeon told me that I may need a colostomy. Now alarmed, I instantly prayed, "Oh ... No, Lord! I do not want a colostomy.

Please heal me in the name of Jesus. Have mercy, Lord." Quick as a flash, I was whisked away to the operating room.

In the operating room, the first person introduced herself to me as my nurse; her name was Mercy. She said she would be attending to me while I was in surgery.

Meanwhile Wiley, my husband, had joined me by now, and he noticed another nurse from a church we attended 30 years ago, named David. Wiley called David by name and then he came into my presence and was with me in the operating room. He held my hand and prayed a sincere anointed prayer for me that the surgery would be successful, and that Jesus would heal my body.

That was the last thing I heard before lights went out for me; I was under anesthesia.

Infection was removed from my body and the surgeons examined every inch of my intestines to determine where the leak or hole was that caused the feces to spread into my body. The leak could not be found. And the conclusion was that my intestines sealed itself.

Hallelujah! Thank you, Jesus! Blessed be Your name forever!

So, now an NG tube (Nasogastric tube) was inserted. You ask, what is an NG tube? A nasogastric tube is a thin, flexible plastic tube that's used for temporary medical purposes.

"Nasogastric" means "nose to stomach".

The tube is designed to pass through your nasal cavity into your throat and down through your esophagus into your stomach. Healthcare providers use different types of nasogastric tubes to deliver substances to your stomach or draw substances out. I dubbed it, "my nose hose".

Thursday, October 4, 2018:

Day 2

NURSE COMFORT...JESUS CAN WORK IT OUT

The name of my day nurse was Comfort. Indeed, Comfort was my comfort that day. Comfort attended to me and nursed me with tender loving care. Melanie, my loving daughter, called me and played and sang the original tune, "Jesus Can Work It Out". Melanie and I were in the church choir and used to sing that song back in the day, which was about 34 years ago.

We reminisced about the joy of choir singing. This song was one of the church favorites. It had a toe-tapping, hand-clapping, lively beat, and spirited rhythm. Precious memories, how they linger. They are kept in the vault of our heart and rise up every now and then.

I went to sleep with that melody and the chorus ringing in my head. "I turned it over to the Lord, and He worked it out. Oh,

Yeah! 🎵 Night fall and the lights are dimmed, but there is a light coming in the room from the hospital corridor. My room was located at the back of the hall. I was in isolation. Nobody but the fully covered masked nurse would be coming to my room.

In the stillness of the night, the moans and groans of painful and lonely patients waft through the halls with an uneasy eeriness. I tried to find a comfortable position while sleeping with the "nose hose." "Jesus can work it out." 🎵 With that melody ringing in my ears, I drifted off into a restful and much needed sleep.

I started dreaming that I was back in a church worship service. People were standing around the altar waiting for prayer for healing. I dreamt Stephani, Melanie's daughter, was an altar worker. As people received prayer, the Holy Spirit would move upon them, and they would fall backwards. Stephani was catching people as the Holy Spirit moved upon them.

I saw the Holy Spirit move over them like a wave, and they were falling down like dominoes. Stephani would catch them, carefully lay them down, and quickly move to the next person before they would fall. It was like I was watching a movie in fast motion. It was so funny. I woke up laughing.

"A happy heart is good medicine, and a joyful mind causes healing." **–Proverbs 17:22 (AMP).**

I thanked God for His Word, for His Promises.

"A happy heart is good medicine, and a joyful mind causes healing."

–Proverbs 17:22 (AMP)

Friday, October 5, 2018:

Day 3

NURSE PATIENCE ...
"I WILL NEVER LEAVE YOU NOR FORSAKE YOU"

The name of my nurse was Patience. By this time, I was seeing what the Lord was doing to assure me of His presence and that He was with me. As it is written, *"I will never leave you nor forsake you."* –**Hebrews 13:5.**

I asked Patience if the nurses made up their names, because the nurses I had in succession were, Mercy, Comfort, and Patience. Mercy was in the emergency room. Comfort was for the first day after surgery. And today is Patience. Each name was a message from the Lord for me.

When I asked Patience if her name was made up, she shared with me that her older brother, 6 years older, named her because he liked a girl in his class named Patience. Okay? Yes, I needed patience as the anesthesia was wearing off and the nose hose (NG tube) was very annoying and extremely uncomfortable. It connected to another hose about 10 ft. long that sucked the bile from my stomach in a container on the wall.

This hose was so long I could jump rope with it. Whenever I had to use the commode, the nose hose had to be disconnected from the 10 ft. suction tube. My sleep was interrupted with pain, blood draws, blood pressure measurements, temperature, and respiration treatments. I thanked God for giving me Patience.

I had a surprise and much-needed visit from my dear friend, Coopie. Wiley, my husband, was her high school teacher in Indiana nearly 50 years ago. Coopie later became my children's babysitter. (My children fondly call her Aunt Coopie.) A few years later, I hired her as my assistant at City Hall in the Comprehensive Employment Training Act, aka CETA program. We also attended the same church and sang in the choir in the Alto section. We sat next to each other in the choir and worshipped, praised, and shouted together. I fondly call her sister friend.

When we moved to California, she came to live with us for a season, and now she lives in Moreno Valley, has a prestigious career, a thriving business, and an active ministry.

Coopie entered the room with Patience, dressed in the gown, mask, and gloves, completely covered, as I was in isolation. She stood patiently observing all that the nurse was doing. I thought she may have been a hospital employee also. I did not recognize her until she spoke. Isn't it wonderful that we all have our own identity in our voice? Oh, my goodness, what a comfort and a joy! Her visit was to witness what the Lord was doing in my life. Coopie was a blessing to me. I was encouraged.

Linda and Gwin, my faithful and good friends, came to visit me and brought beautiful flowers. We sang, "Waymaker" and worshipped the Lord. Because I was in isolation, Linda and Gwin were covered with a gown, mask, and gloves. As we worshipped the Lord, He met us there in the midst. My spirit was lifted. I was blessed by their presence.

That night, the song, "Waymaker", continued to ring in my ears. 🎵 Waymaker, Miracle Worker, Promise Keeper, Light in the Darkness, my God, that is who You are.

I felt as if the Lord was saying, "I see you." (El Roi, The God who sees me.) And I was saying it back to Him, "I see You"… (in the names of my nurses).

I was reminded of the testimony of Hagar and Ishmael when she was banished from the household of Abram by Abram's wife, Sarai. Hagar was the handmaid of Sarai, and she conceived a son, Ishmael, from Abram. Sarai at that time had no son. Hagar taunted Sarai with the fact that she had a son and Sarai was old and barren. Of course, this caused tension and conflict between the two of them.

Sarai dealt with Hagar harshly, to Hagar and Hagar fled to the desert with her son, Ishmael. Alone in the desert, hungry and thirsty, Hagar was prepared to die with her son. Hagar was in the desert by a spring of water when the Angel of the Lord came to her. He prophesied to her about Ishmael and told her to return to Sarai and submit to her. Hagar gave the name of the Lord, EL ROI, the God who sees me.

–Genesis 16:13-14. NKJV

Now I am aware and very interested in how the Lord is using the names of the nurses to minister to me. The name of my night nurse was Serena. I looked at her and smiled saying, "Oh, you come in peace." She smiled back and nodded. Yes, I needed peace at night. Prayers were going forth that my bowels would move. I had sounds of movement. My bowels were sleeping and needed to wake up.

And she called the name of the LORD that spake unto her, Thou God seest me: for she said, Have I also here looked after him that seeth me? Wherefore the well was called Beerlahairoi; behold, it is between Kadesh and Bered.

–Genesis 16:13-14 (NKJV)

Saturday, October 6, 2018:

Day 4

JASMINE... "PYT" (PRETTY YOUNG THING)

The nurse for the day was Jasmine, a sweet-smelling flower, and the charge nurse was Rosa, another fragrant flower. God sent me flowers. I see His hand of mercy and grace. The thought that God brought me living flowers put a smile on my face.

After lying and stewing in my own sweat for four days with no water or food in my mouth, nor water on my body, a bath was most welcoming and needed. Kimmie and Jasmine washed my body while still in the bed. A song burst forth from my spirit, "You Make Me Feel Brand New", by the Stylistics. My body was fresh and clean. The lyrics of another song, my adult children, Melanie and Michael, introduced to me came to mind. "Ain't nobody dope as me, I'm just so fresh and so clean. So fresh and so clean, clean," by the singing group, OutKast. These lyrics made my heart sing.

Jasmine was so young and quick. She would ask me a question three times, before I could answer. I nicknamed her "PYT".

A Michael Jackson song, "Pretty Young Thing". She liked it and we immediately became friends. Jasmine nursed me back to health with excellency. Pastor Curtis and Joyce Levi, pastors of United Prayer Power Fellowship, came to visit and prayed with me. I was inspired. I started walking to wake up my bowels. The name of the night nurse was, Christian, the way of life.

Strength and honour are her clothing; and she shall rejoice in time to come.

–Proverbs 31:25 (KJV)

Sunday, October 7, 2018:

Day 5

GOD'S GRACE

Pastor Dorothy Porter, pastor of Prayer and Praise Church Of God In Christ (COGIC), and a retired Registered Nurse (RN) of 40 years came to minister and serve me Communion (the meal that heals). I saw her coming as she walked into my isolation room.

Her radiance filled the doorway as she entered. She was dressed in all white. She was smiling and looking like an angel. We worshipped the Lord in song; we prayed, and I received the bread which represents the broken body of Christ. I drank the juice which represents the precious blood of Christ. I received it in faith. This is the first crumb and taste of juice since Wednesday.

NPO was posted above my headboard. What does NPO mean, you ask? NPO means "nothing by mouth," from the Latin, "nil per os". It is doctor's shorthand. I was still on NPO. Nothing by mouth—not even ice chips—nada. Nevertheless, I took

Communion and received in faith. 🎵 Waymaker, Miracle Worker, Promise Keeper, Light in the Darkness, was our song of worship. I was concerned about my recovery to health. When would my bowels wake up and start moving?

How long would I have to stay in the hospital? Pastor Porter spoke a word into my life. She said, "No hurries, no worries. God has you in His hands. There is no hurry. There is no worry." That word gave me peace. I trusted God and I rested assured He has a plan for me. *"For I know the thoughts that I think toward you, says the Lord, thoughts of peace and not of evil, to give you a future and a hope."*
–Jeremiah 29:11 NKJV

After Pastor Porter left, it was back to walking back and forth down the hospital corridors to help my bowels move. All was going well, until the "nose hose" became disconnected. I left a trail of green bile like a snail that leaves its slimy track. Yuck!

My nurse in training that day was Gloria. The unexpected disconnection caused Gloria and me to spontaneously work together. We bonded on the floor that day. Gloria urgently coaxed me to get back to the room as I left a trail of green bile behind us. Now back in my room, Gloria began changing my gown, reconnecting the hose, and making me comfortable. At the time, I could not see anything glorious about what just happened. The day is not over.

Yes, the meal that heals was received that afternoon. Just a few hours later when the nurse's shift changed, I was transferred from Isolation to the Medical floor. I was moving on up to the 5th floor. I am a step closer to going home. Oh, now, I see, GLORY!

Okay, I was moving from the Isolation, which was a huge room approximately 15 ft. by 20 ft., and I was the only patient in the room. N0w, I was moving to a shared room and my bed was next to the door that opened to the hallway.

My luxury penthouse suite (aka Isolation) was reduced to the size of a shared closet. I felt a bit disoriented. The change was so swift. What few possessions I had were quickly gathered and placed on a cart. So, down the corridor and into the elevator we traveled.

I'm still in the hospital bed with the nose hose and all its contraptions, the cart with a bottle of grape juice, Matzo crackers, and flowers, and away we paraded to the 5th floor. It left my head swimming as to what was happening. Things were so different on the 5th floor. I kept reminding myself that I was on my way home. Thank you, Lord. This night, the nurse was Grace. I see you, Lord.

Monday, October 8, 2018:

Day 6

THE SUNFLOWER...
PRECIOUS MEMORIES

It's a new day. I'm in a new room on a different floor, and I had a small bowel movement. Yeah! Thank you, Jesus! I started walking down the corridor and found the Visitors Room at the end of the hall. I entered into this room with raised hands and sang a song. You know which one? 🎵 Waymaker, Miracle Worker, Promise Keeper, Light in the Darkness: My God, that is Who You are. 🎵 I sanctified it with worship, praise, and prayer. I called it my sanctuary.

On the 5th floor, I could look out over the city and see that God was in control of everything and everybody. As the traffic moved along the 10 Freeway, it was very clear to me that God is present. He is everywhere, touching hearts, healing bodies, mending brokenness, changing lives, and performing miracles. Oh yes, God is Sovereign.

Sylvia and Anthony came to visit bringing gifts and flowers. Among the flower arrangement was the Sunflower.

The Sunflower has a story from my childhood. I lived on farm in Indiana where my father planted and harvested corn and soybeans. One year, the fields would yield soybeans and the next year corn, and so forth. The year that soybeans were planted, some of the corn seeds from the previous year would spout up along with Sunflowers and thistles.

During the summer, my brothers and my sister would take to the back 60 acres and cut down the corn stalks, Sunflowers, and hoe out thistles. We had corn knives and hoes that we sharpened on a spinning stone wheel. Before we went to the fields, we sharpened our corn knives and hoes, watching the sparks fly, and made sure our blades were shiny and sharp.

Off to the field we would go early in the morning after a hearty breakfast. Mom had prepared cold water in thermos and would come to pick us up before it got hot around noon. We knew the plan. When we saw a Sunflower, with one swift swing and a shout, the Sunflower would fall. HiYah! It was like chopping down a tree, and it was the same with the corn stalks that were now weeds in the soybean field. HiYah! They would drop to the ground. We were helping Dad. The Sunflower and corn stalks would tear up the combine at harvest time, and they had to go.

Now on Saturday, the family would go to town and visit my Grandma, my mother's mother. I was so surprised to see Grandma growing Sunflowers in her garden.

"What?! Grandma, you're growing Sunflowers; they are weeds!" Grandma explained to me that Sunflowers follow the sun. In the morning, they face the East to greet the rising sun, then they turn their heads to the sun and follow it as it travels across the sky. I had a new perspective of Sunflowers because of my Grandma. What a pleasant memory brought to mind by a simple gift of the Sunflower. Thank you, Lord, for making me smile.

Sylvia, Anthony, and I visited in the sanctuary until the nurse came to take me back to my room. God blessed me again with friends, gifts, and the precious memory of the Sunflower.

Tuesday, October 9, 2018:

Day 7

PUSHING THROUGH THE PAIN—"STRONG & FAST"

June was my nurse today. Oh, June represents summer, the beach with the sound of the waves crashing on the shore, the smell of salty air, the seagulls croaking to one another, sunny days, picnics, parks, BBQs, golfing with Wiley, children laughing and playing. I'd watched the kids jump over the waves and build sandcastles. Some would dig holes in the sand to catch sand crabs and place them in a bucket; others would look for seashells to gather.

Watching the waves and the people was entertainment within itself. Yes, the great Pacific Ocean at my back door in sunny Southern California, my home. I was abundantly blessed. Thank you, Lord, for pleasant memories. I could almost feel the warmth of the sun and the smell of the ocean in this cold sterile hospital environment. I en- joyed being outdoors and loved Nature, God's creation. I saw beauty everywhere.

My sisters, Denise and Sheila, sent me their smiling faces through the phone. It was so comforting. It made me smile to see friendly, loving, familiar faces. Sending me their smiling faces was like the faces of angels guarding and giving me peace. **Numbers 6:24.**

Later that afternoon, I was walking with Wiley, and I was pushing through my pain. "Just one more lap," I would say. He walked with me each time, entering the sanctuary at the end of the hall, worshipping and thanking the Lord for His goodness and faithfulness. When I returned to the room, I grimaced because of pain and fatigue.

He watched me push through the pain and he encouraged me with these words: He said if I were on his football team, he would make me a "safety". I asked him, "What does a safety do?" He said, "The safety is strong and fast. The safety makes more tackles than the linebacker. He is very intuitive and runs the secondary defense."

After being married for 49 years, Wiley gave me one of the best compliments. Oh, these words made my heart swell and my spirit soar. The love of my life said I could be on his football team as a key player. WOW! Thank you, Wiley, for seeing my character and speaking to my spirit. I was overjoyed with tears.

"The Lord bless you and keep you.

–Numbers 6:24 (KJV)

Wednesday, October 11, 2018:

Day 8

GOD KEEPS HIS PROMISES

Still no water and no food. Amazingly, I was not hungry. The IV was feeding me fluids, antibiotics, potassium, and magnesium. My bowels were still sluggish, so I decided to call my son, Michael, to tell me something funny so I could have a good belly laugh; thinking a good belly laugh would help activate my bowels. Well, it worked (kind of). I laughed so hard that the nose hose became dislodged and fell out onto the floor!

To my surprise, I looked at this gross tube lying on the floor and wondered, "Now what?"

An X-ray had been ordered and the technician was on the way up to my room to see if the NG tube was placed correctly. My output from the nose hose had been so great that the doctor was beginning to wonder if the NG tube was in the right place. And now I have laughed it out. What's next? What's going to happen now?

Well, another NG tube had to be inserted. By the look on the nurse's face, it looked like this might be an unpleasant procedure. The first NG tube was placed while in surgery and I was under anesthesia. It was simple because there was no gagging reflex. I was asleep then. Here it is eight days later, and I am wide awake and no anesthesia.

I told the charge nurse who was going to insert this NG tube that I was an athlete, and she was my coach. Coach Maura told me what to expect and what I was to do, and this procedure would be easy as pie. I watched her measure the distance from my nose to my stomach and cut the tube accordingly. She told me when to take a small sip of water to help facilitate moving the tube down to my stomach. I was praying.

Yes, the NG tube went down with ease, no gagging on my part. Coach Maura was beaming, and I was happy that the Lord blessed us and made it easy. Thank you, Jesus. She gave me a "high 5". This day was dubbed as "training day". My head coach was Wiley, who has been my daily support and comfort. X-rays were taken and it was determined that the newly inserted NG tube was in the correct place. Yes, my output was reduced to half the bile.

Wiley and I met another patient, Christo, who told us his testimony of God's protection and healing. Christo, and his wife,

Pearl, and his daughter, Crystal, told us how God kept him and brought him through a heart attack.

While we were in the sanctuary, we heard an amazing testimony of God's grace, again. Christo explained that his name means little Christ. His wife's name, Pearl, means a gem of great value, and Crystal, his daughter's name means transparent joy. His whole family was there sharing the love of God in his testimony. Our hearts were made glad. And we marveled at his testimony.

He talked about how he would go fishing on the pier at 5 o'clock in the morning. The seals would often take the fish as he reeled them in. He would literally be fighting the seals to keep his fish! He would share his catch with his neighbors.

It was an amazing story. He was so physically exhausted from fishing and gathering the fish, putting them in the bucket, carrying them back to his truck and walking back along the pier. He could barely drive home.

He was so close to having a heart attack, but God had mercy on him and spared his life. His wife brought him to the emergency room, and it was determined there that his heart was under great stress, and he was admitted to the hospital.

Later that day, the Smith's came and showered me with flowers and gifts. Lavender Gladiolas, reminiscent of my mother's flowers on the farm in the front by the road, blush roses in a beautiful turquoise mirrored vase, more roses and Freesia in another turquoise mirrored vase perfumed and decorated my room. An extraordinary, eye-popping, lilac moon stone Orchid, a true showstopper, was a real gem. Everyone who came into my room marveled at its beauty.

My room looked like a flower garden … so colorful and fragrant … and absolutely beautiful. The Smiths generously and abundantly loaded me with gifts, lavender scented soap, Seascape fragrance, and gift cards from Cheesecake Factory and Red Robin. Oh, my goodness gracious. I was so blessed as they demonstrated the love of God.

Because I had no water or food for ten days, my olfactory nerve was extremely sensitive. The blue plastic gloves were smelling toxic, and all the nurses had to wear them. Putting on the gloves was one of the first things they did as they entered the room. The drill was: enter the room, reach for the gloves that were mounted on the wall, and proceed to my bed. It was one swift move.

Aside from the smell of the blue plastic gloves, the smell of the blankets made me nauseous. The lavender scented soap was heavenly. I thanked the Smiths for their generosity. They were the hands and feet of Jesus. We went to the sanctuary and talked and visited. Oh, what joy filled my heart as we shared sweet memories and talked about the goodness of God.

Later, Wiley joined us and we prayed and thanked God for my healing. We were all in agreement knowing that God keeps His promises. *"For no matter how many promises God has made, they*

are 'Yes' in Christ. And, so, through him, the 'Amen' is spoken by us to the glory of God."
–I Corinthians 2:20

Thursday, October 12, 2018: Day 9

JESUS... THE LIGHT OF THE WORLD!

Today was a productive day. The green bile had decreased dramatically. My bowels were moving more frequently. I still had no water and no food, but things were about to change. Prayers were being answered. My body was responding positively.

My faithful friends, the Levi's, came to visit, and we went to the sanctuary. They prayed with me and shared the word of God. Pastor Curtis shared how the Lord delivered him of pain. We praised the Lord and thanked Him for His healing power. His testimony was encouraging and was like the proverbial "shot in the arm."

I decided that my way out of the hospital and my way home were linked to my walking and my worship down in the sanctuary. Each time I walked to the end of the hall, I entered the sanctuary and worshipped the Lord.

Sometimes I would rock in the rocking chair and sing praises and pray. Then I'd start walking again to return and do it all over again.

For my bowels to wake up, I decided I would go walking regardless of the time. Morning, noon, or night, I went walking. I was on a mission. I'm walking my way home! Oh, how precious was that time of healing and worship. God honored our time together. A hymnal melody wafts to my mind, "🎵 Walk in the light, beautiful light. Come where the dewdrops of mercy are bright. Shine all around me both day and by night, Jesus the Light of the world".

Again Jesus spoke to them, saying, "I am the light of the world. Whoever follows me will not walk in darkness but will have the light of life."

–John 8:12 (ESV)

Friday, October 12, 2018:

Day 10

GOD ALREADY WORKED IT OUT!

Hallelujah! The nose hose was removed! I am free from that waggling, annoying, and disgraceful NG tube. The accompanying hissing and whizzing of the hose—gone! I began looking normal again. The humiliating nose hose that was attached to my face and the container that collected the fluid from my stomach—gone! Oh yes, out of sight! Free at last, free at last, thank God Almighty, I'm free at last!

At noon, I was given a liquid diet. No vomiting. Everything tasted delicious. Ice chips and gelato were my favorites, and yellow lemon Jell-O was oh, sooo good. Next meal was solid food for dinner. As I was wondering what Wiley would eat for dinner, there was an extra dinner tray, and it was offered to Wiley. Wiley and I ate dinner together. While I was trying to figure it out, God had already worked it out. The provisions of God are continuously available, a never-ending supply.

All is well. I see going home in my near future. Thank you, Lord, for answering our prayers, and bless all the people who have been praying for me. Grant them the desires of their heart. Give them peace.

And we know that all things work together for good to them that love God, to them who are the called according to his purpose.
–Romans 8:28 (KJV)

Saturday, October 13, 2018: Day 11

HOME AT LAST!

Oh, happy day! It's 8 a.m. and I hear the wheels on the food cart rolling down the corridors. Oh, now, this time the sound stopped at my room. Could it be that the food cart had a delivery for me. Oh, yes, what a welcome sight, and the aroma of a tasty, long-awaited breakfast was so inviting. I had a good, hearty breakfast with scrambled eggs, lightly toasted bread, and a pat of butter, strawberry jam, oatmeal with a carton of low fat 2% milk, and apple juice. It was quite satisfying.

The doctors have agreed that I can go home. After the second NG tube was inserted, the output was reduced to half. And it was determined that the NG tube inserted in surgery was in the Duodenum, and not in the stomach. Dr. O was right. The NG tube was incorrectly placed.

Michael's hilariously funny story caused me to laugh the NG out and it fell out on the floor. Yes, it was a blowout, to the Glory of God!

Oh, the wisdom of God is past our finding out. I love Him and I trust Him. As it is written, "O the depth of the riches, both of the wisdom and knowledge of God! How unsearch- able are his judgments, and his ways past finding out!"

–Romans 11:33

Glory to God in the Highest! Bless the Wonderful Name of Jesus!

Home at last! Getting ready for bed was so welcoming. Freshly laundered sheets that smelled like lavender, and a customized pillow cradled me like a newborn baby. My soft, comfy PJs replaced the string ties in the open-backed hospital gown. There were no interruptions from a phlebotomist with blood draws. There was no crying and moaning from troubled patients, nor blaring loud intercom paging.

Tranquility filled my bedroom. A soft glowing light and silence lulled me to a peaceful sleep. I was home in my bedroom and lying next to my faithful husband, head coach, and best friend. I had a good night's sleep. Thank you, Jesus. The Lord is keeping his eyes on me.

"He who watches over you will not slumber"; indeed, he who watches over Israel (Marsha) will neither slumber nor sleep.

–**Psalms 121:3-4**

And He continues to keep me and is still watching over me.

October 2019 Time to Downsize

TIME TO DOWNSIZE

Wiley and I woke up in the morning. And it was as if he had a dream and wanted to tell me about it.

He said, "We going to move."

My response: "Okay, to where are we moving?"

Wiley: "We're going to move to Arizona."

Me: "Okay, when are we moving?"

Wiley: "We're going to start getting ready now."

Well, this did not seem completely out of the blue. We had a timeshare in Scottsdale, and we invited Melanie and Michael and their family each year for family bonding and vacationing. Now it was Fall 2019.

Our children were grown and had families of their own. We were empty-nesters, retired, and living in a two-story home with four bedrooms, 2-1/2 baths. We had talked about downsizing, and it was time to act on it.

Behold, I will do a new thing, Now it shall spring forth; Shall you not know it? I will even make a road in the wilderness, and rivers in the desert.

–Isaiah 43:19 (KJV)

November 2019

God's Plan Works Best

GOD'S PLAN WORKS BEST

We began emptying our home of accumulated stuff we had gathered over 30 years. We had an estate sale, gave to Goodwill, friends, neighbors, and filled three dumpsters of stuff. We placed our house up for sale in November 2019.

It was surprising that people came to our house on Thanksgiving to look at the house. My thought was Thanksgiving is a holiday, and people had a day off and just wanted to check it out. Wiley was home, but I was visiting my sisters in Fresno. It really was not an inconvenience since there was no Thanksgiving meal prepared in our home. Our house was clean with no food odors to distract potential buyers. We had more than 20 interested families to come and view our home. But nobody was making any offers.

sAt that time, we were also looking for a home in Arizona that was close to where our son, Michael, and his family lived.

Michael and Kimberly, his loving wife, kept telling us to look into this active senior resort on the golf course. We were reluctant because of the HOA (Home Owners Association), and we had not been paying an HOA in California. However, after scouting the community, we put in a contingency bid for a home.

We were waiting for our home to sell before we could purchase another home. And in the meantime, the AZ owner died, and the daughter was managing the estate. This plan did not work out. The bid for the house fell through. In retrospect, it was all in God's plan.

For I know the thoughts that I think toward you, saith the Lord, thoughts of peace, and not of evil, to give you an expected end.

–Jeremiah 29:11 (KJV)

December 2019

True Acts of God

TRUE ACTS OF GOD

It was during the Christmas holiday that my sister's home was broken into at night by a thief. Christmas gifts purchased for her staff and wrapped presents were visibly placed outside her bedroom, and they were passed by. It was as if they were invisible.

While my sister was sleeping with an open door to her bedroom, the thief stole her computer and ate bananas. He left the banana peels on the dresser in the front bedroom where he exited as if to signify, "I was here".

Although her purse was open and money was exposed, no money was taken. Sheila slept undisturbed. I believe the angels were standing guard and she was cloaked. When the thief left the house through the front bedroom window, the alarm sounded and woke up my sister. The police came and recorded the theft.

Thank God for protecting my sister as she slept soundly while the thief was roaming through her house. Not a hair on her head was touched.

The good Lord was hiding her, her purse full of money, and the wrapped Christmas presents. Hidden treasures in plain sight. Yes, God was watching over her, protecting her, keeping her from all danger and harm. Bless His Holy Name. Psalm 91:1-5: "He who dwells in the secret place of the Most High shall abide under the shadow of the Almighty. I will say of the Lord, He is my refuge and my fortress; My God, in Him I will trust. Surely He shall deliver you from the snare of the fowler and from the perilous pestilence. He shall cover you with His feathers, and under His wings you shall take refuge; His truth shall be your shield and buckler. You shall not be afraid of the terror by night".

While visiting with my sister, I shared with her the house that caught my eye, and I really liked it. This house was special in that it had everything we wanted in a house, and it was on a golf course. In addition, the house street address had the same name of my sister, Sheila. And it was within two miles of Michael and Kimberly's home. The only obstacle was the house was above the price range that Wiley and I had agreed upon.

I made a statement of faith to Sheila stating that it would be an act of God for us to purchase this house. We prayed and asked the Lord for His wisdom and guidance.

Romans 11:33: *"Oh, the depth of the riches both of the wisdom and knowledge of God! How unsearchable are His judgments and His ways past finding out"!*

I John 5:14: "Now this is the confidence that we have in Him, that if we ask anything according to His will, He hears us. 15 And if we know that He hears us, whatever we ask, we know that we have the petitions that we have asked of Him".

January 2020

It Was My Voice...It Was Me!

IT WAS MY VOICE....
IT WAS ME!

It's another new year and we are looking forward to a change in location and a new home in Arizona where we'll be living close to our son and his family.

There was a lump found in my thyroid, and a biopsy was taken. The biopsy was inconclusive regarding whether it was benign or malignant. Surgery was scheduled for January 2020.

Surgery was performed and my thyroid was removed because the lump was malignant. The cancer had moved into my air duct and vocal cords.

Waking up still heavily sedated from the surgery, I noticed that my hands were tied down to the bed and there was a pipe taped to my mouth. I heard over the speaker that I was in intensive care. WHAT? I was shocked by this announcement. What happened?

Why was I in intensive care? Questions bombarded my mind. I was conscious only for a few minutes and immediately slipped back into a deep sleep.

I dreamt that it was snowing. Snow was falling into my room from an open ceiling. Snow covered my head, my blankets, the table, the medical equipment, the doctor, my husband, and everything that was in the room. Everything was covered. It was like a blanket of snow covering everything. Everything and everyone were white with snow. I heard the Holy Spirit speak to my spirit, "Marsha, you are covered. Everything will be all right". Thank you, Lord, for giving me peace.

The next morning, Wiley and the surgeon entered the room and explained to me what happened. My thyroid was removed, and reconstruction was performed on my windpipe and vocal cords. The pipe was placed as a precaution in case I was unable to breathe after the reconstruction. Now I was conscious, the pipe was removed, and my hands were untied.

Looking intently at Wiley and my doctor, she said that I could speak. In my mind, I thought, "What would I sound like? Would my voice be the same? Would it be a whisper? Would it be raspy? Would I be able to sing?"

The only way for me to know was to speak. So, my first words spoken were, "Good Morning." Oh, my goodness gracious! It was my voice that I have always known. There was no change in pitch or volume. It was me. Thank you, Lord! Several days in the hospital and I was released to go home.

February 2020

The GREATEST of These Is LOVE

THE GREATEST OF THESE IS LOVE

Further treatment was six weeks of radiation at Hoag Family Cancer Institute located in Newport Beach. The route to Newport Beach was through the winding Canyon and onto the busy freeway, through to the Orange Crush. It was named the Orange Crush because several of the freeways merged right there at the Angel Stadium.

Once you pass the Orange Crush, the route continued to go South headed towards the beach. It would normally take 75 minutes to travel because of the congestive, hustling traffic. However, because COVID was just in full swing, there was hardly any traffic on the freeway, so the trek down to Newport Beach was cut in half. It was 35 minutes. We cruised down the freeway void of traffic jams listening to our favorite jams. Thank you, Lord.

Wiley and I would park our car down at the beach and watch the waves come in. Because the beach was closed, there was NOBODY at the beach. We had our pick of parking places right up front in the parking lot at the beach.

We would park and watch the waves as they were perpetually rolling in. I started to think about the goodness of God and His promises and attributes.

I would name the waves that were coming in. They were coming in from the deep, bringing me the blessings of God. So, as the waves rushed in, I'd say, "Here comes healing. Healing is coming to me in Jesus' name." And what would I want to throw onto the wave as it returned back to the deep? I would cast the cancer on the wave back into the deep.

"Healing come; cancer go."

Next, peace came rolling in, and I would cast anxiety onto the wave going back. 1 Peter 5:7: "Casting the whole of your care all your anxieties, all your worries, all your concerns, once and for all] on Him, for He cares for you affectionately and cares about you watchfully". –Amplified Bible (AMP)

Comfort would come, and what would I put in comfort? I exchanged frustration for comfort. Then, this wave came that was so powerful—rushing and crashing into shore. I could see it billowing up—building and building—getting closer and closer. It was mountainous. I said, "Oh, my goodness! What wave could this be?

What is coming in to me?" And I heard in my spirit: "That's the love of God coming towards you."

Love, His uncompromising, unconditional, all inclusive, never ending, powerful love enveloped me and swallowed up all my fears, cares, hurts, pain, and sorrow. I sensed His love washing over my spirit, and the peace of God that transcends all understanding is what remained.

Five days a week, Monday through Friday, for six weeks, we traveled down to our private beach and the cancer center for radiation treatments. What could have been laborious and stressful, God gave us a window of tranquility looking out over the aquamarine waves with white caps rolling up into a frothy foam. What a glorious sight. Yes, there is blessed peace in the turbulent storms of life.

May 2020

Divine Connection

DIVINE CONNECTION

During those six weeks, we took our house off the market. My health and well-being were my priorities. I wanted to concentrate without distractions or interruptions.

After the radiation treatments were completed, we placed the house back on the market. The house sold within one week. Wow! Now, the ball was rolling again. I had asked my daughter-in-love, Kimberly, to go look at this house that I had my eye on back in December. That was the house on Sheila Lane. The owner of the house had taken the house off the MLS, which is the multiple listing, so it wouldn't be viewed online.

I asked Kimberly, "Will you look at this house and see if it's still up for sale?" She took a realtor with her to check out the house. It was as if the Lord was hiding it. Huh?

Kimberly and the realtor went to look at the house on Sheila Lane and the report came back: "Mom, this house has your name written all over it!" Kimberly saw a picture of the owner's son and asked the owner if that picture was his son. She called his name and stated that his son and she had attended the same high school together in northern California.

The owner acknowledged that, "Yes", that was indeed his son and that he served in the Armed Forces. We marveled at what are the chances of walking into a house in Arizona where Kimberly knew the owner's son. There was a divine connection. Thank you, Lord!

We made an offer on the house and a counteroffer was made. Lo' and behold, an agreeable price was negotiated, which enabled us to purchase the house. We sold our California home on Friday and purchased our Arizona home on Sunday. We sold and purchased our homes over the weekend. Now, we had 30 days to move from our home in California to our new home Arizona.

How do you pack and move 30 years of stuff within 30 days?! This was an exciting adventure, and we felt the Lord leading and guiding us as we now journeyed to another place.

We filled three big city dumpsters with our belongings. Things that we had accumulated over the years. Stuff packed away and long forgotten. We must have kept the items for sentimental reasons, because they certainly weren't being used. We donated to Goodwill, to friends, and neighbors.

June 2020

A Forever Faithful God

A FOREVER FAITHFUL GOD

Little by little, our belongings were packed, donated, or tossed away. Our four bedrooms, two and half baths, and three-car garage home was completely empty. All our belongings were removed from the house. Clothing, furniture, pictures, kitchen appliances, dishes, silverware, all packed up.

The house was now empty. Nothing remained. It was void of all personal items. The only thing remaining was a broom and a dustpan left in the garage. I shed a tear because we were leaving not just the house, but our home and precious memories, good neighbors, and close friends. It was a kind of loss that I had not experienced before.

Wiley and I prayed in the empty house, standing in the empty garage. We asked the Lord to "bless the family coming to live in this house" and that the banner over this house would be God's love.

The moving van had left. Wiley and I headed to Goodyear, Arizona. Goodbye to California and hello to Arizona. As one chapter ended in California another chapter began in Arizona. Oh, how exciting. Oh, what an adventure.

Yes, Lord, You have already prepared the way. Thank You, Lord, for Your faithfulness. Thank You for watching over us. Yes, Lord, You see me. And I see You!

THE END

Your steadfast love, O Lord, extends to the heavens, your faithfulness to the clouds.

–Psalm 36:5 (KJV)

I See You!
By Marsha L. Jones
Copyright ©2025 by Marsha L. Jones

Edited by Flo S. Jenkins
Words That Flo! ... Editorial Consultancy Services (GoodJenks Media & Publishing Group)
Torrance, CA
www.wordsthatflo.com
Cover Designer: Javohn K Oddie

The Eye Of God is an illustration of the Helix Nebula
Formatter: Javohn K Oddie
All rights reserved. No part of this publication may be reproduced, scanned, stored in a retrieval system, or transmitted, in any form or by any means, electronic, mechanical, photocopying, recording, or otherwise, or distributed without the prior authorized written approved permission of author and/or publisher, except in the case of brief quotations embodied in critical professional reviews and certain other noncommercial uses permitted by copyright law. For permission

requests, contact the author and/or publisher with the subject addressed: "Attention: Permissions Personnel" at email address: jnissij@gmail.com

MEET THE AUTHOR

Just when you think nobody knows what you are going through—a broken heart, sickness, disappointment, or pain— and you are in a place of hopelessness and emptiness, THEN, GOD GIVES YOU A WINK! It's at that exact moment in time, and the precise place where you are, that something so profound happens!

It is not a coincident nor happenstance! You know for sure, without a shadow of doubt, that God hears your prayers and answers your prayers. He knows your circumstances. He knows where you are. He knows what is going on. He is the All-Knowing, All-

Powerful, All-Loving, Ever-Present God Who has His eyes on you. EL ROI, THE GOD WHO SEES ME.

Marsha L. Jones and her husband, the late Wiley Jones, pastored Agape Family Life Center Church in Rancho Cucamonga, CA. She continues to minister the Word of God, while always encouraging others. Marsha is the author and publisher of a children's book entitled, Barnyard Classroom, A Friend. It is a true story about autistic children and shows that everybody has a God-given talent, despite life's challenges.

Marsha presently resides in Arizona.

BOOKS BY THE AUTHOR

Hammy and Packy were the most unlikely pair to become the best of friends. But what they learned is that they had more in common than they realized and their friendship was a match made in the perfect barnyard!

NOW AVAILABLE:
www.amazon.com

www.ingramcontent.com/pod-product-compliance
Lightning Source LLC
Chambersburg PA
CBHW050916160426
43194CB00011B/2436